FAR,
FAR AWAY -
Pocket Edition

V. PEREIRA

DEDICATION

To Gary, my 'baby, baby'....the man who makes all this possible.
And to my long lost friend, Lauri and sister Deanna.
And to Steph, Allstar, Amy, Robin, Duckie, Maria, Mona , and Cindy .
You're all the best!

WELCOME.....

To Auntie V.'s land of Far, Far Away!

I've always been a dreamer with a wild imagination.
And I'm thankful to finally have an outlet for my creativity.
I'm happy to say that this book is my best yet.
I'm really proud of the unique, hand drawn images I
was able to dream up and capture on paper:)

I hope you enjoy coloring these designs as much as I enjoyed creating
them.

"Auntie V."

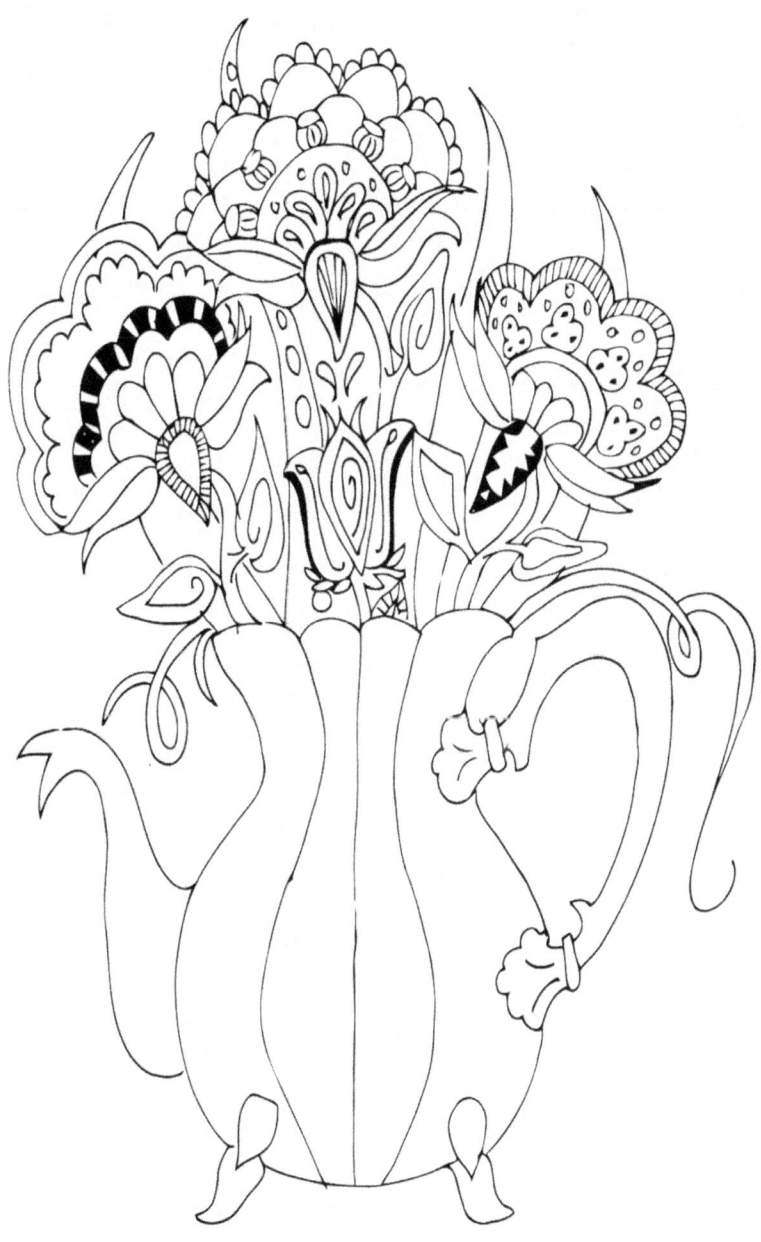

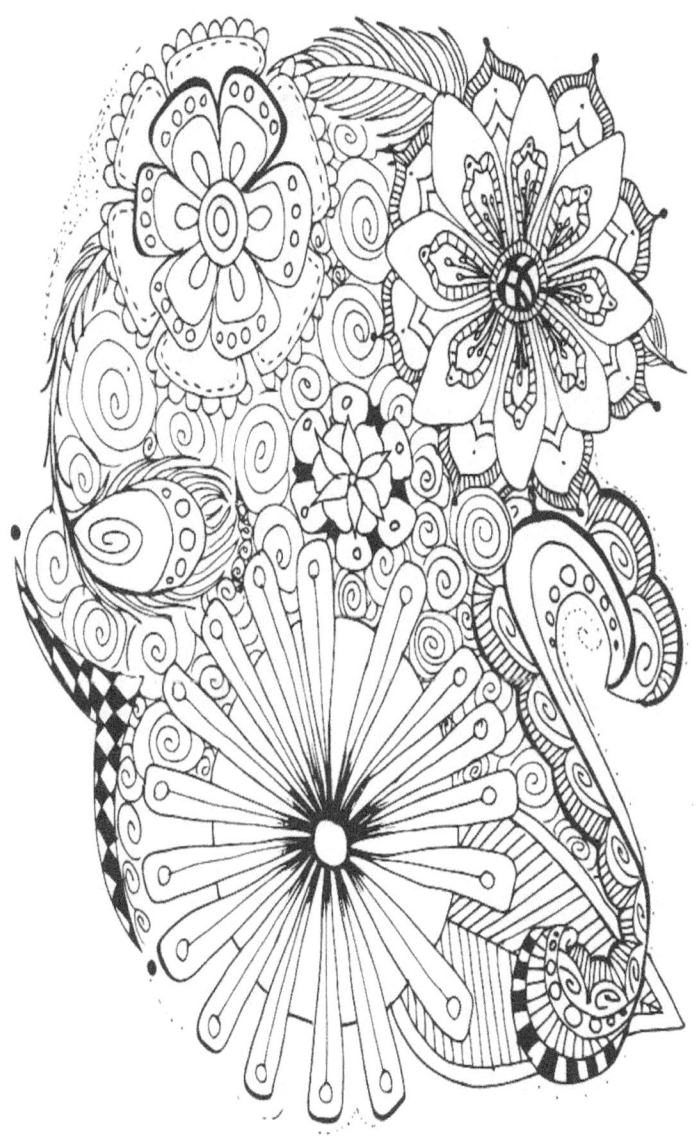

V. PEREIRA

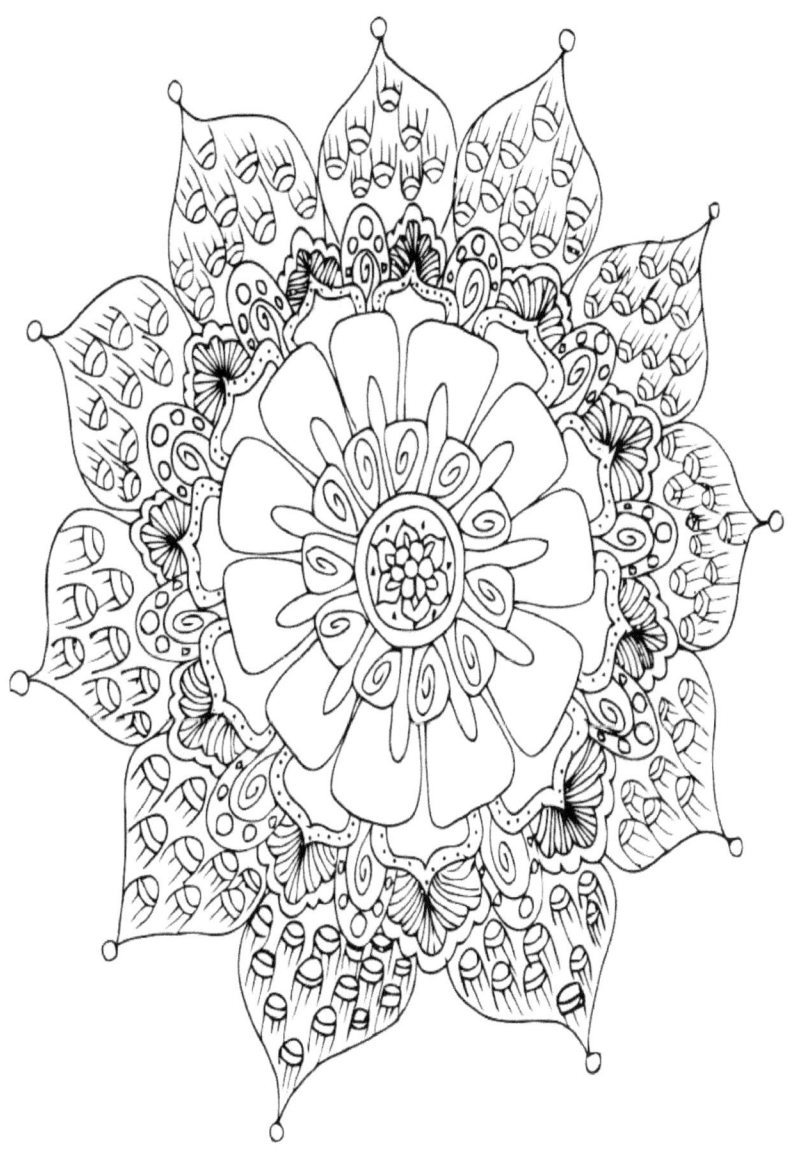

V. PEREIRA

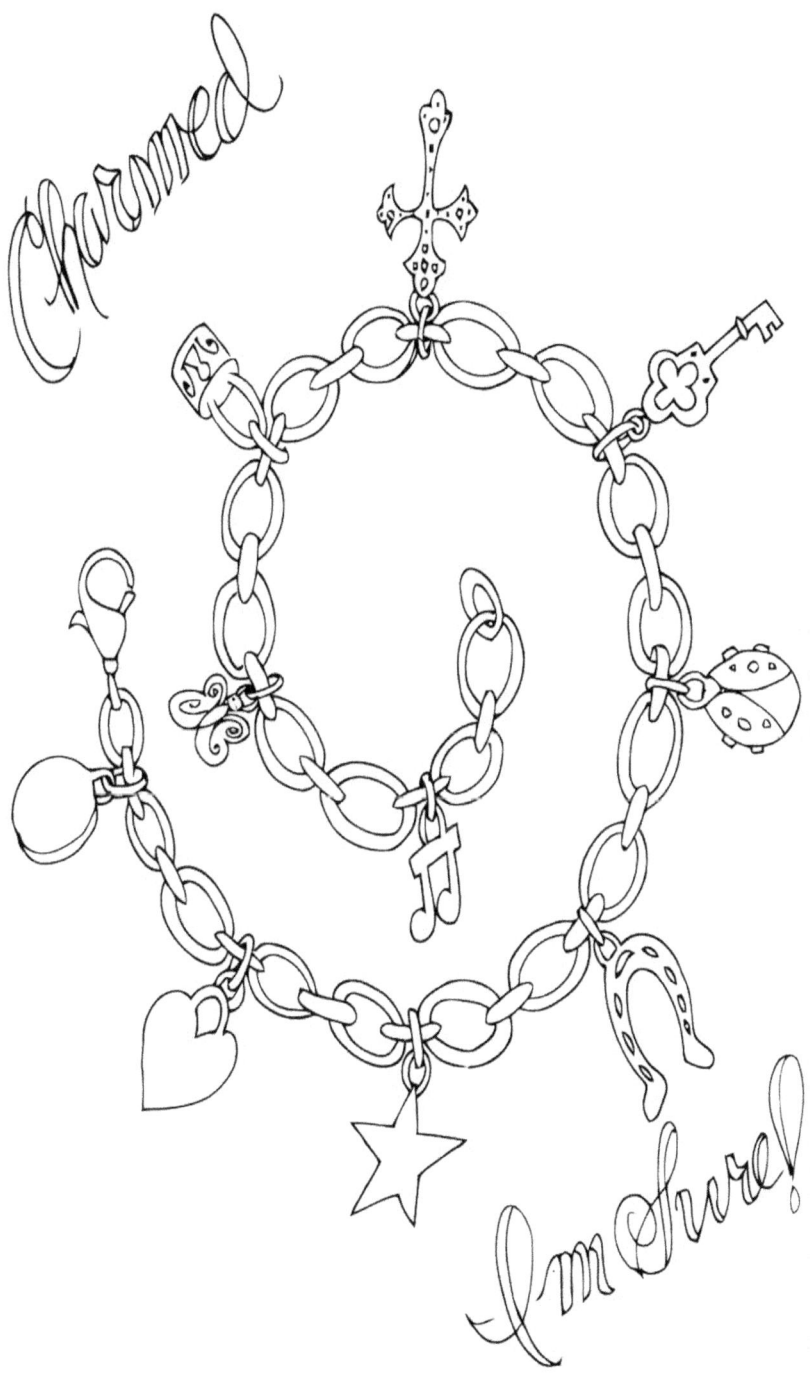

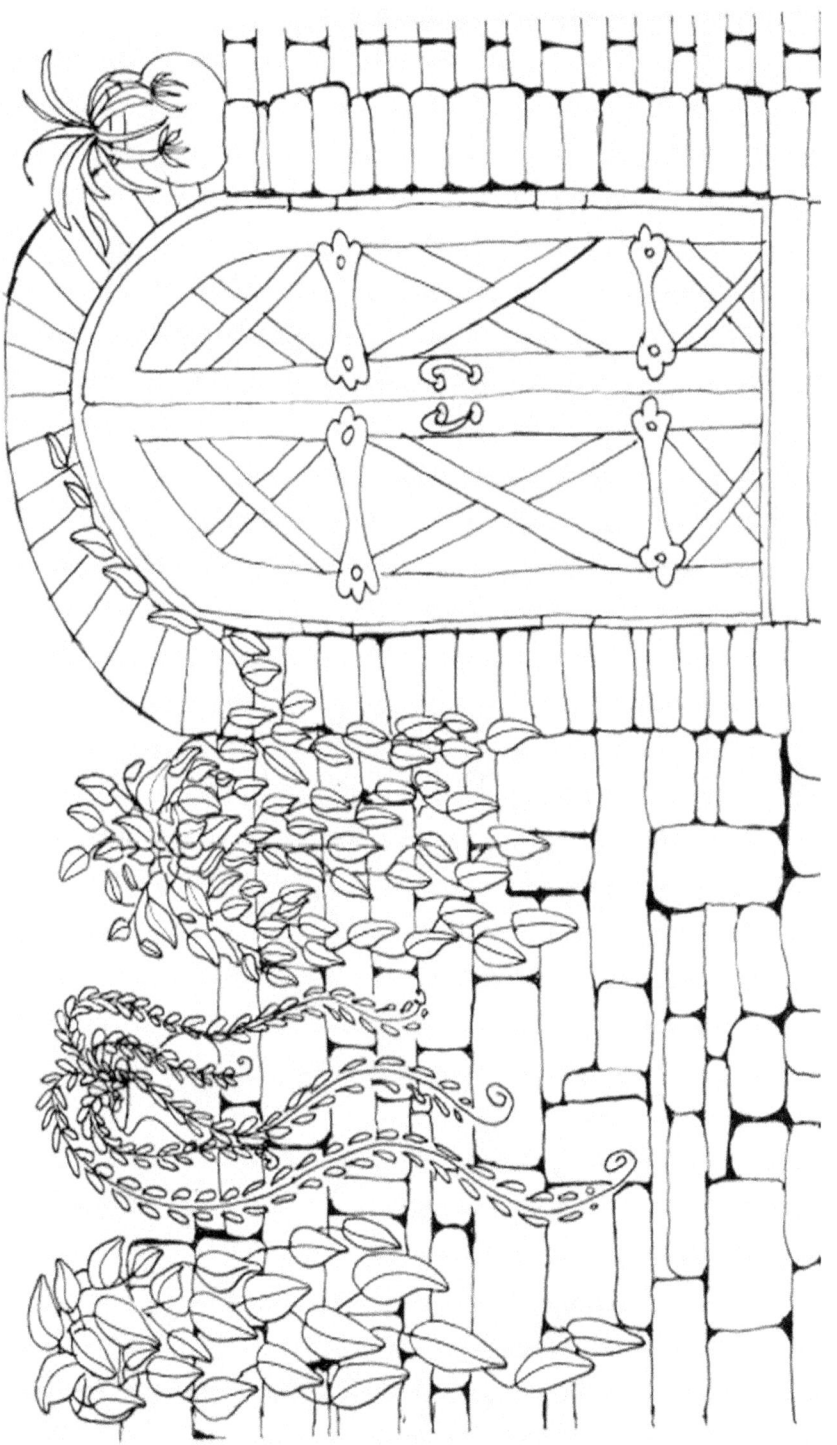

V. PEREIRA

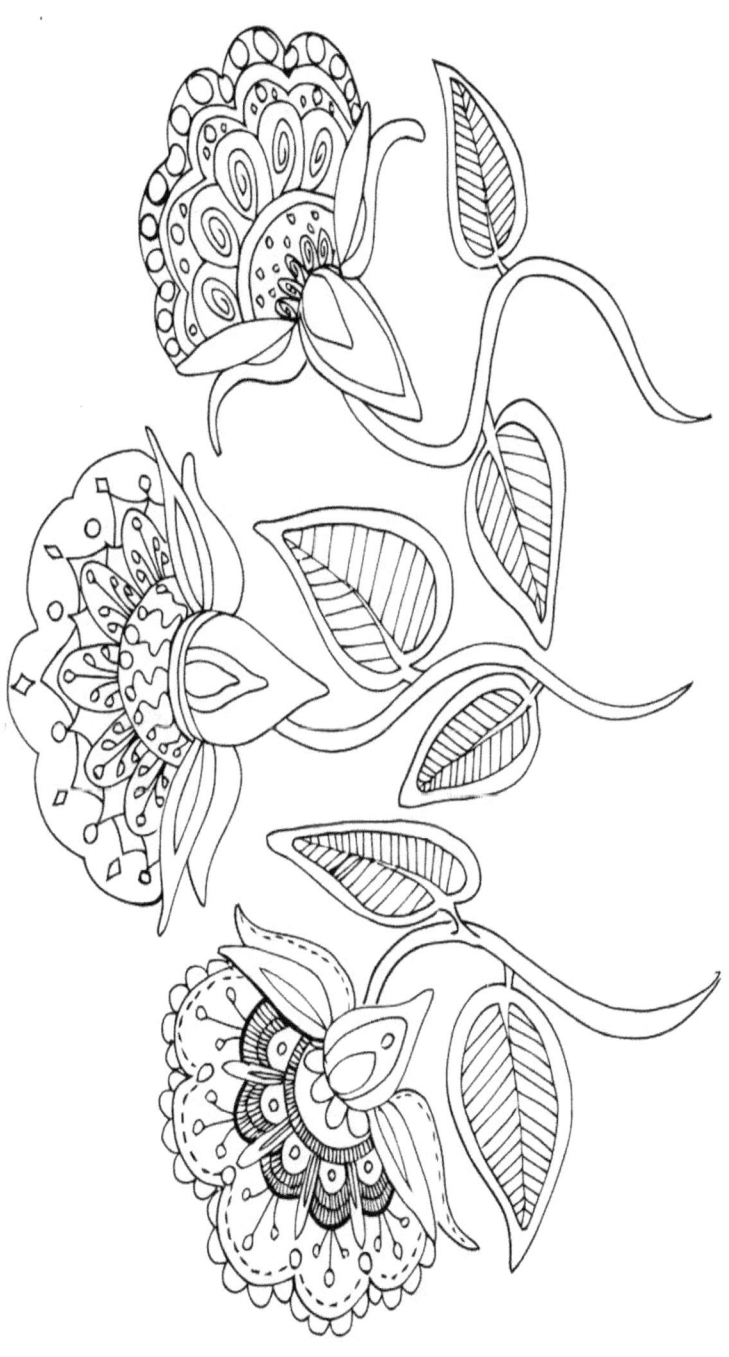

V. PEREIRA

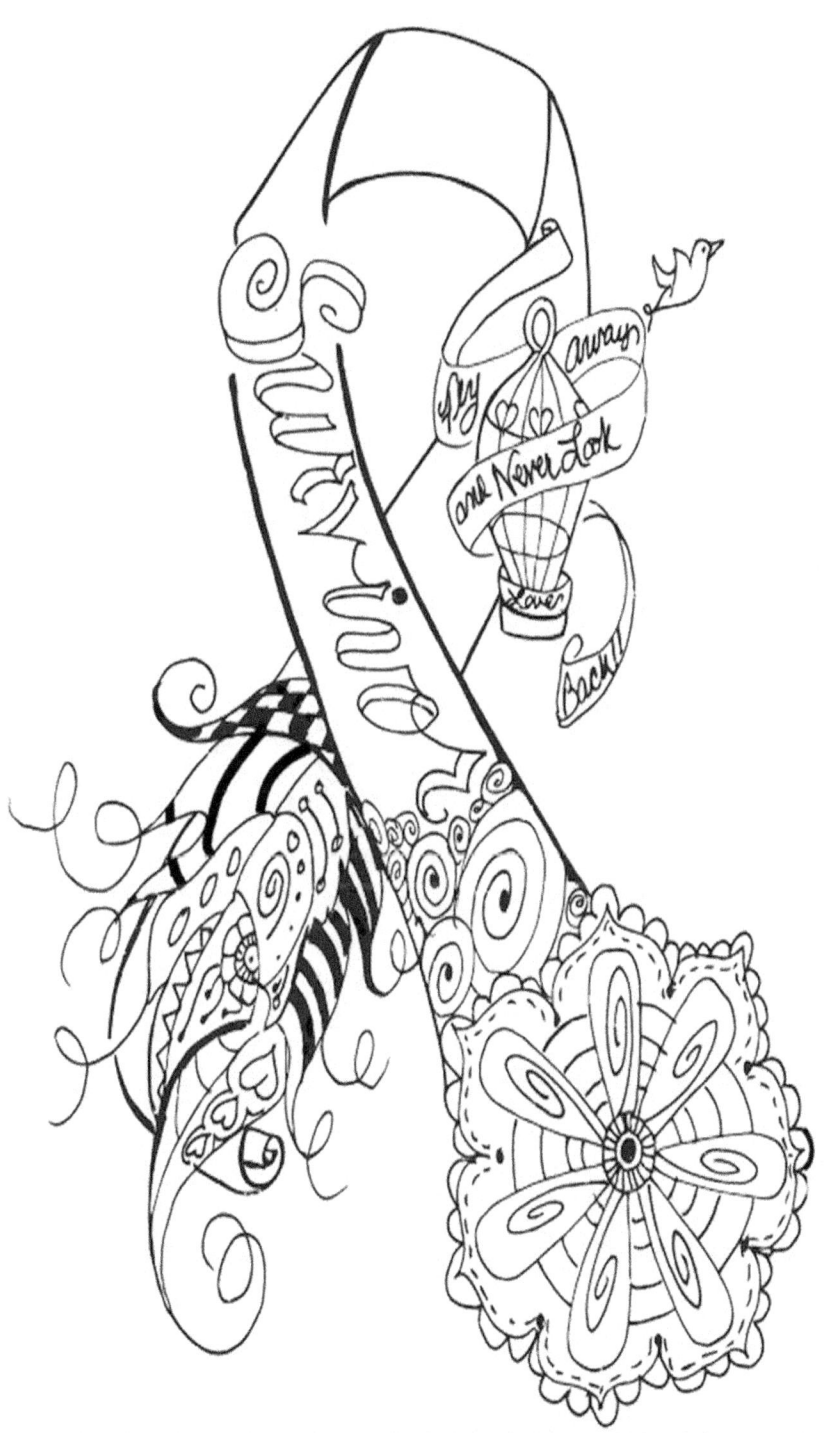

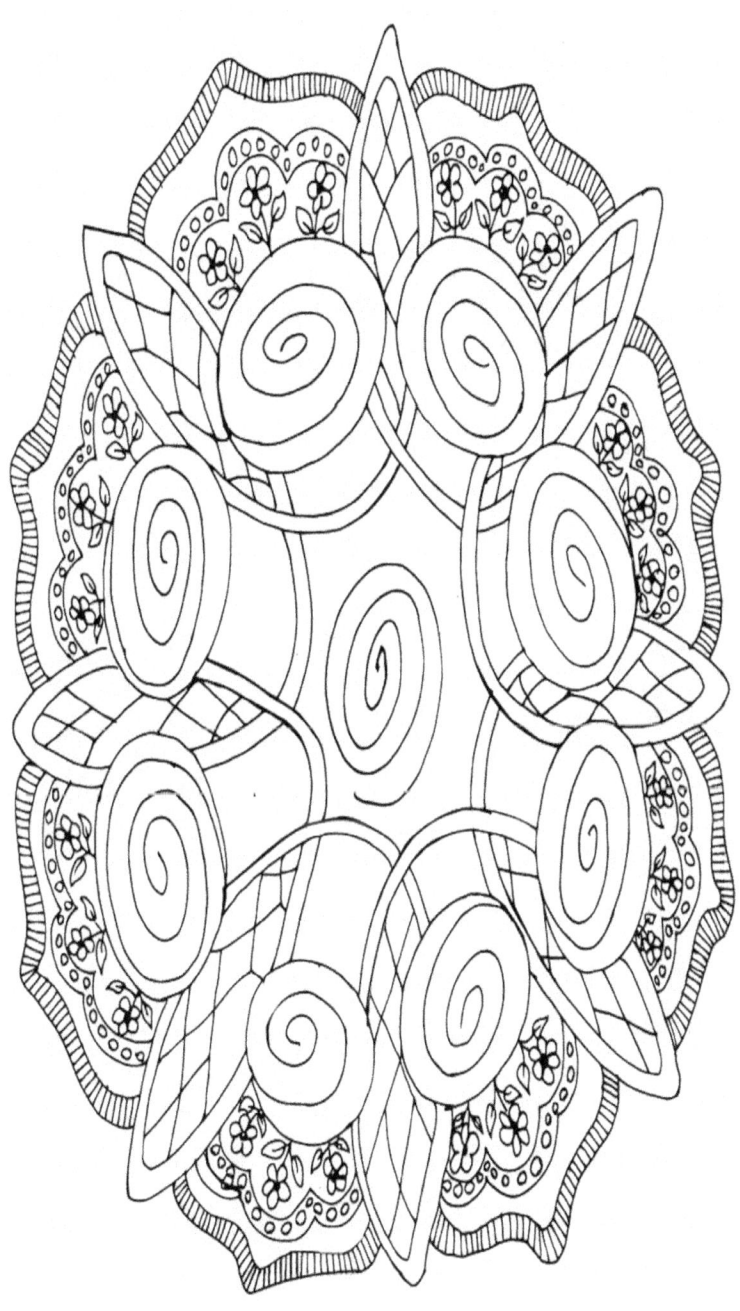

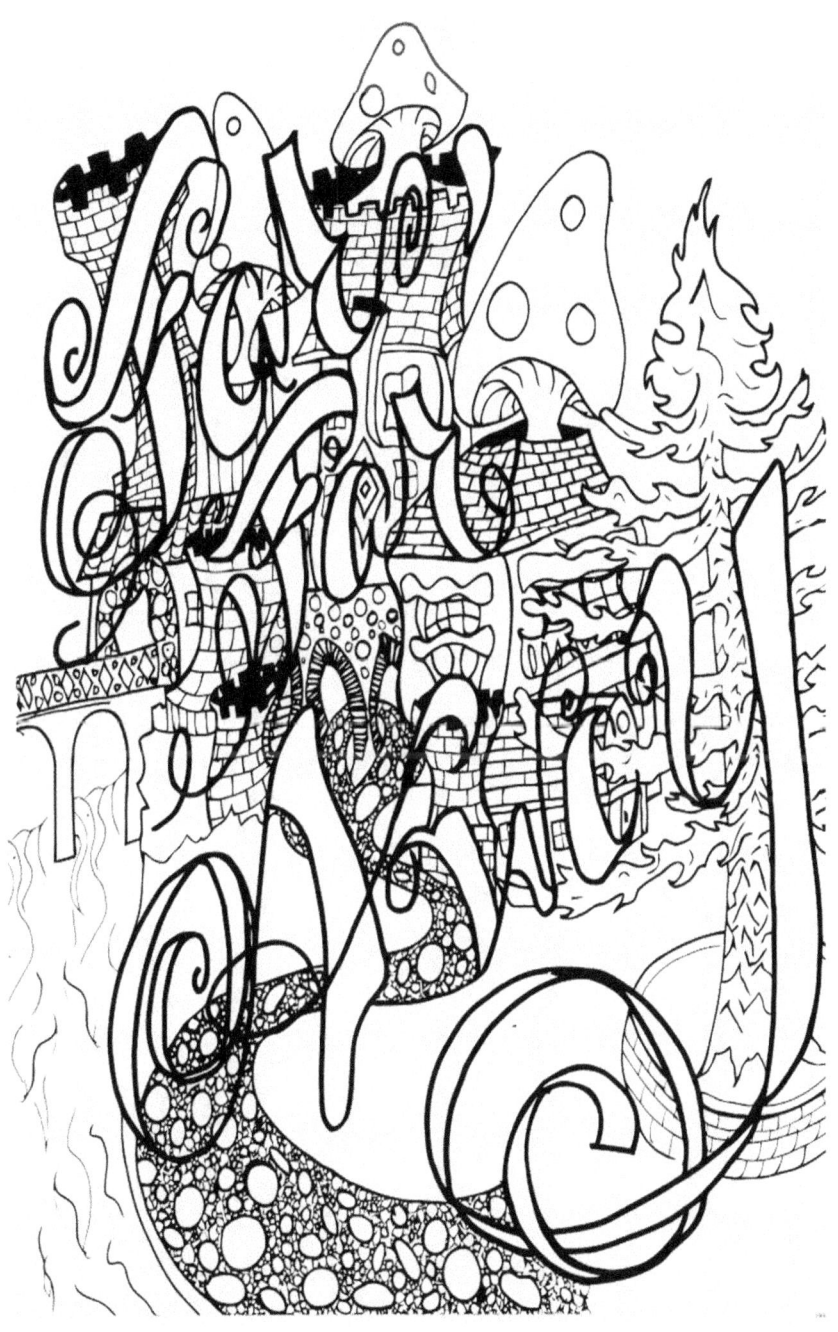

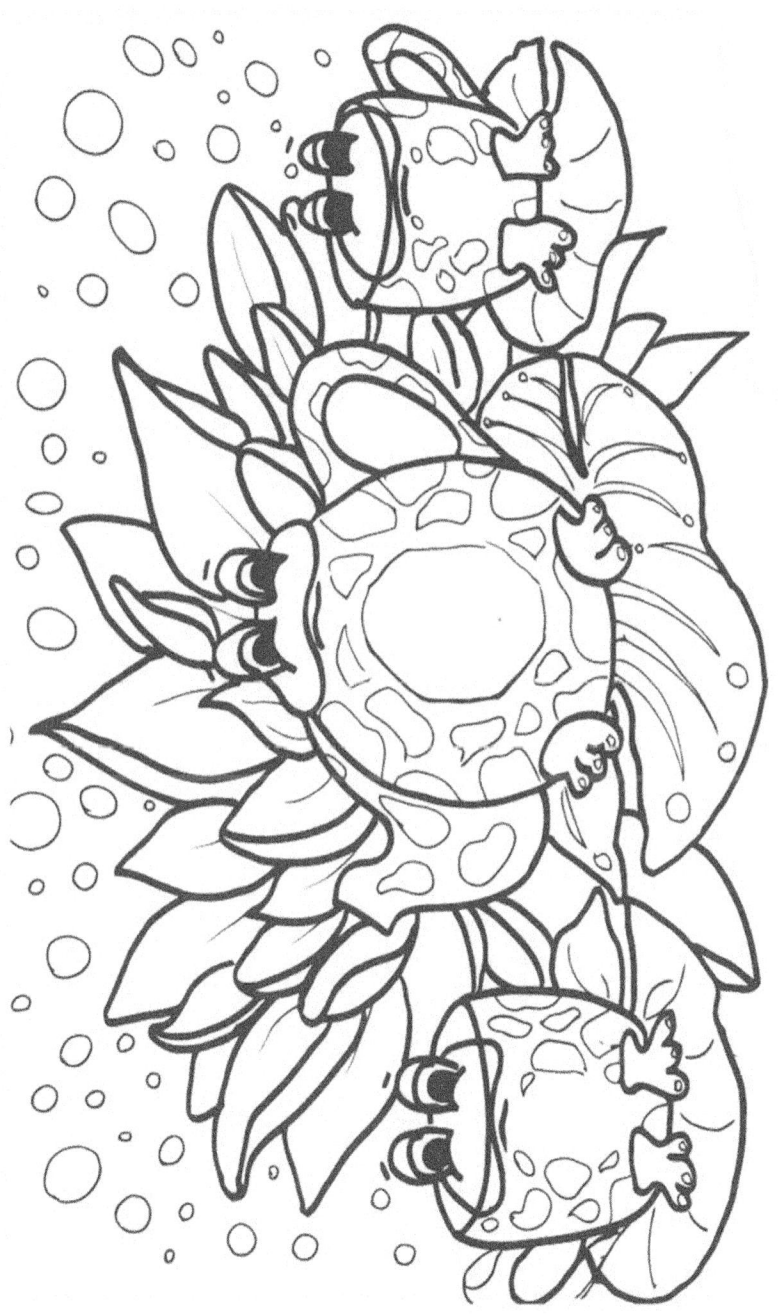

V. PEREIRA

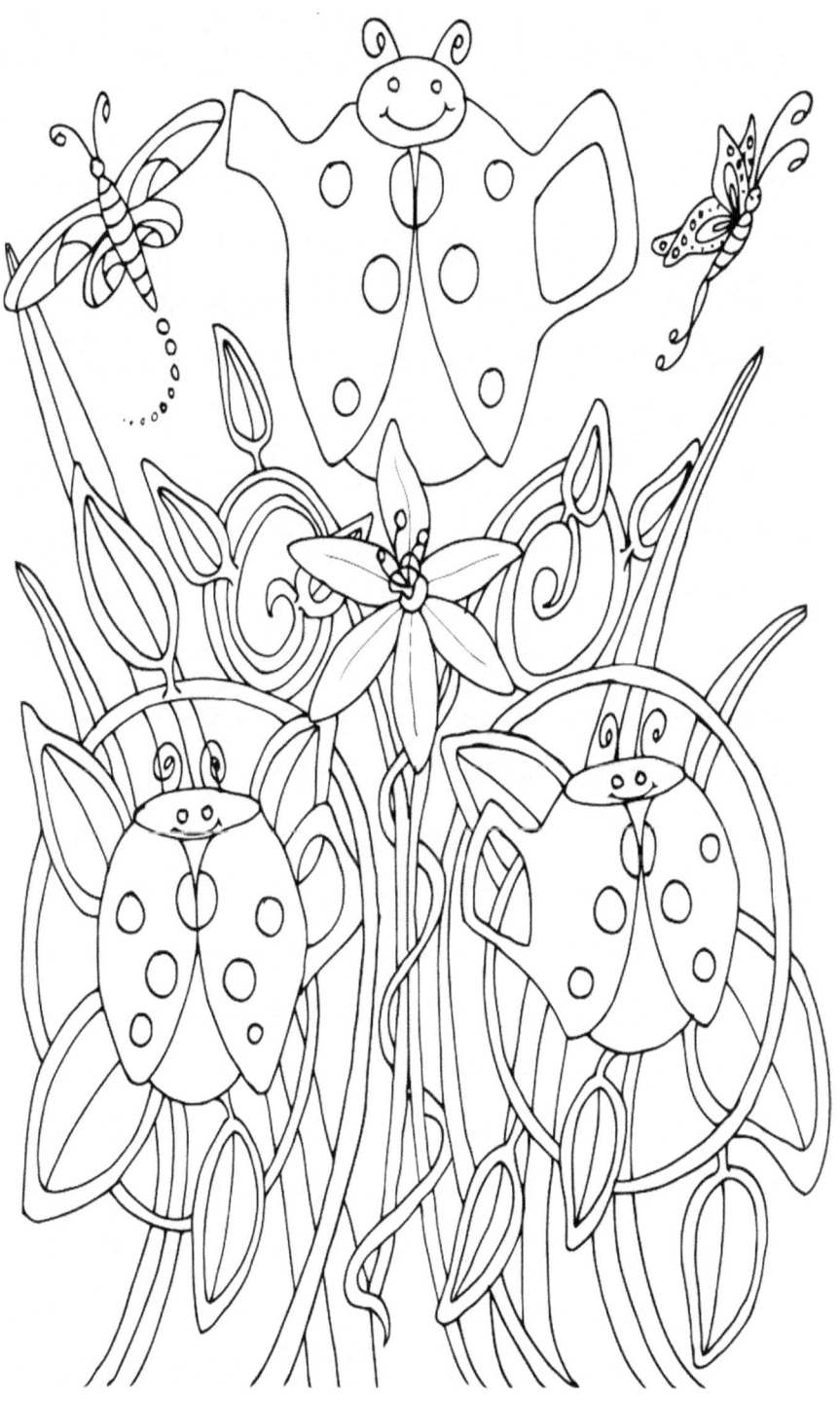

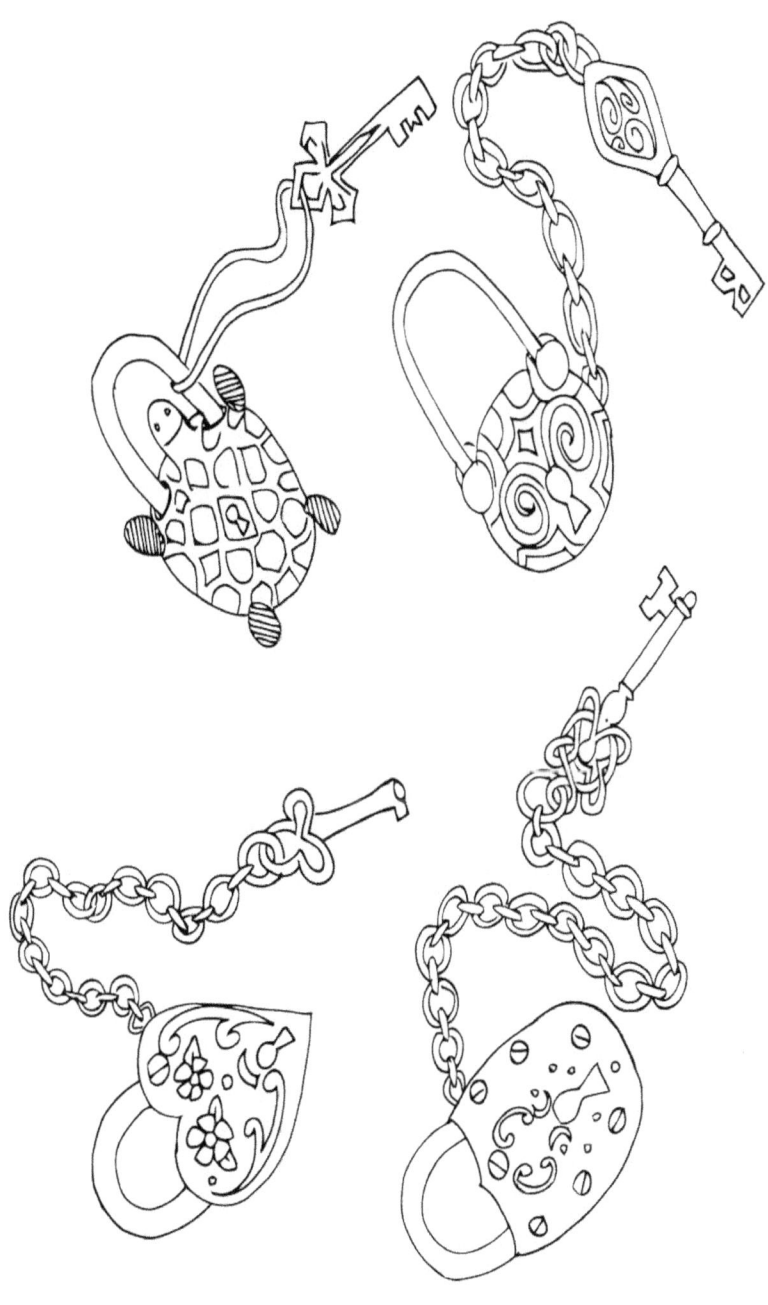

V. PEREIRA

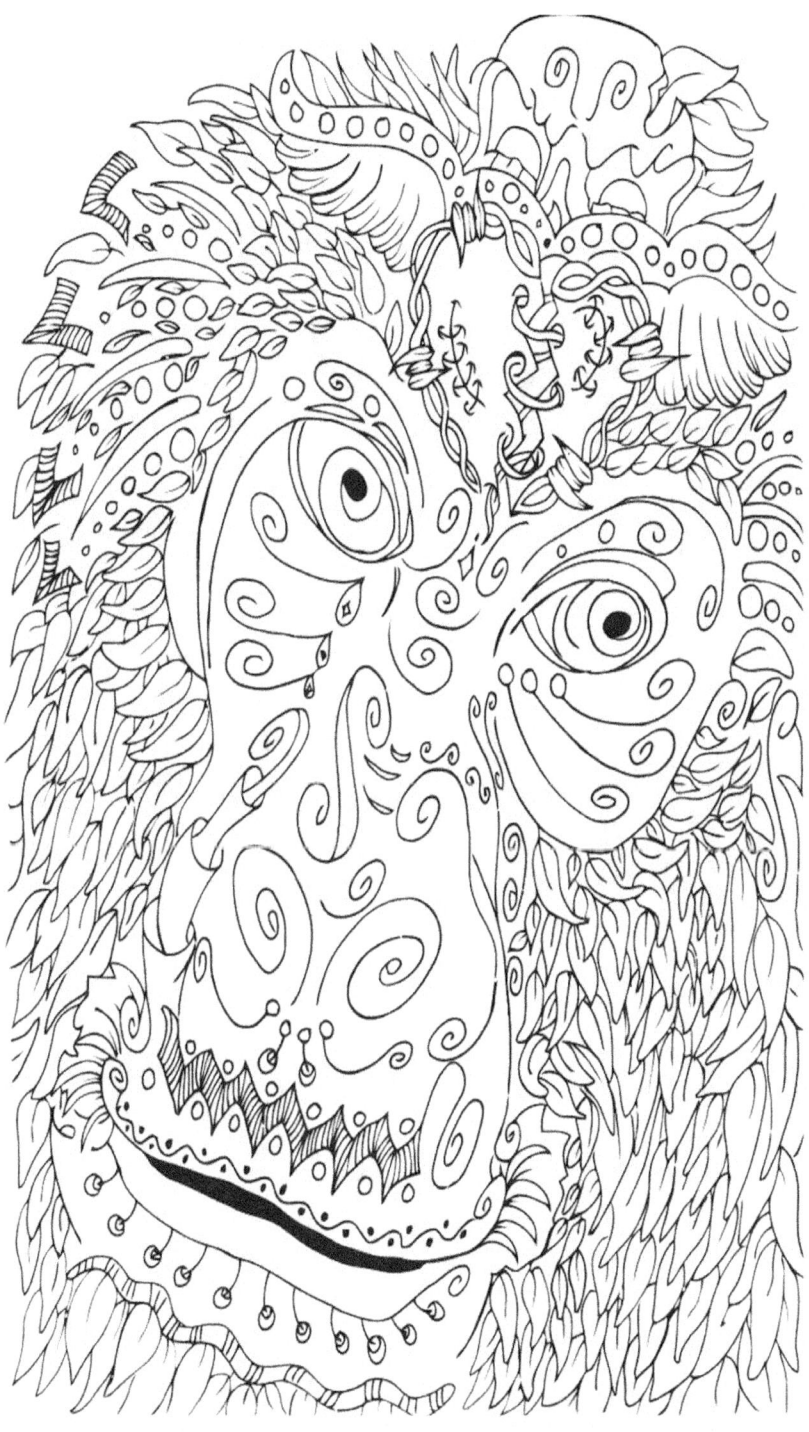

V. PEREIRA

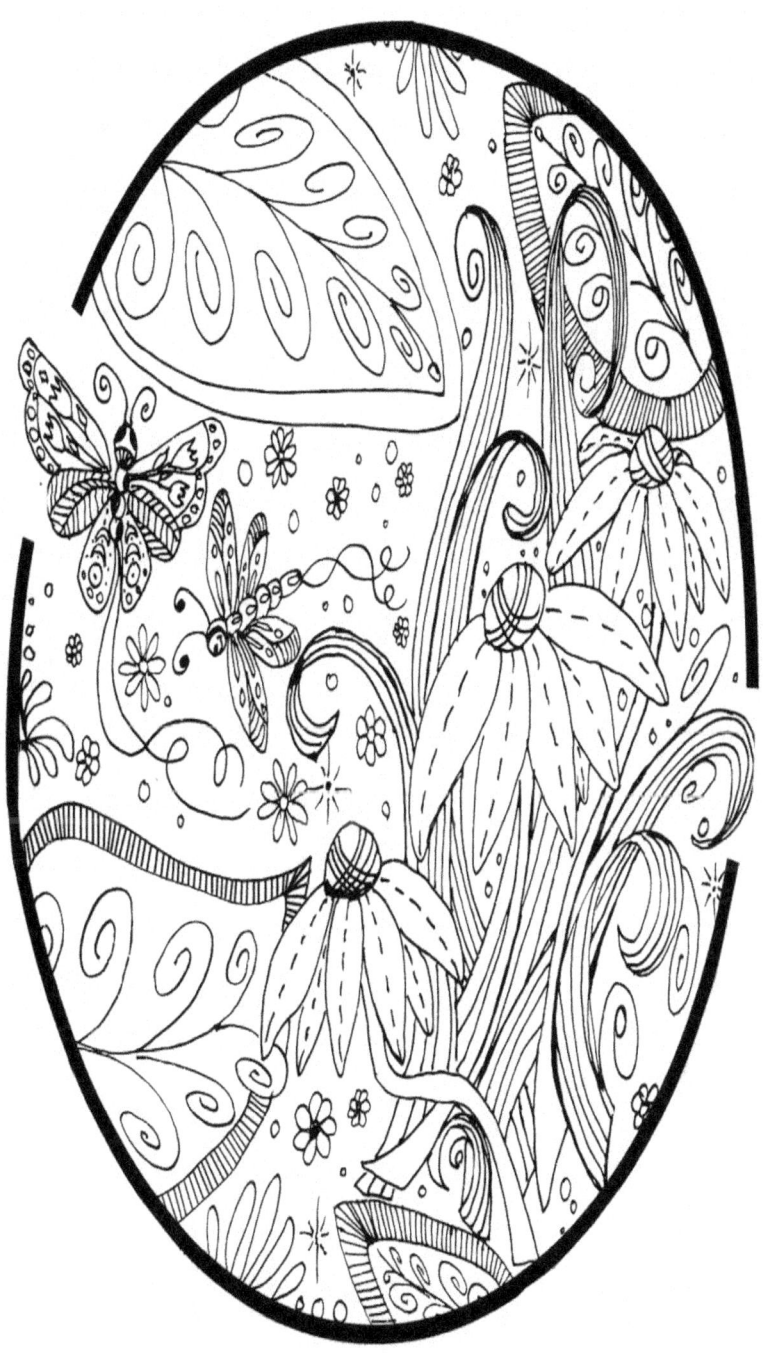

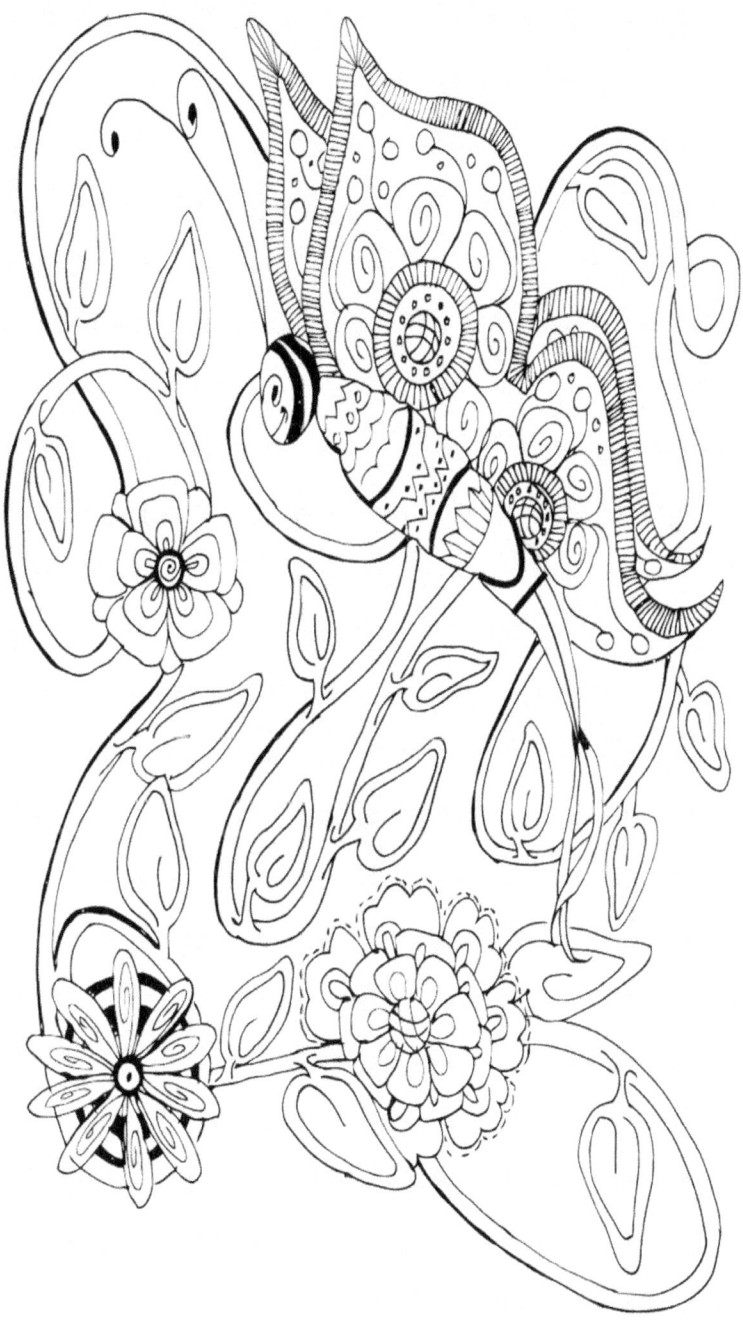

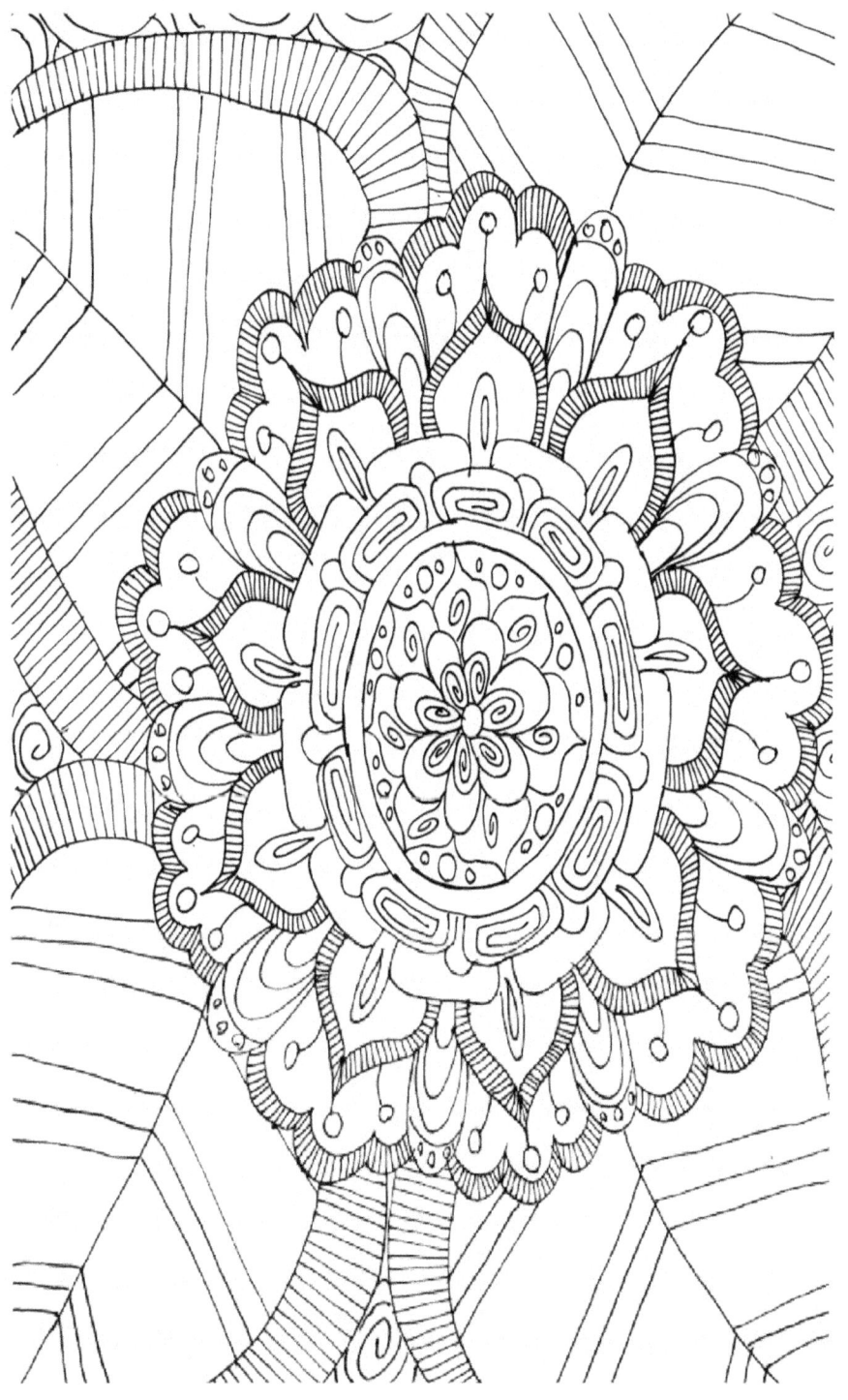

V. PEREIRA

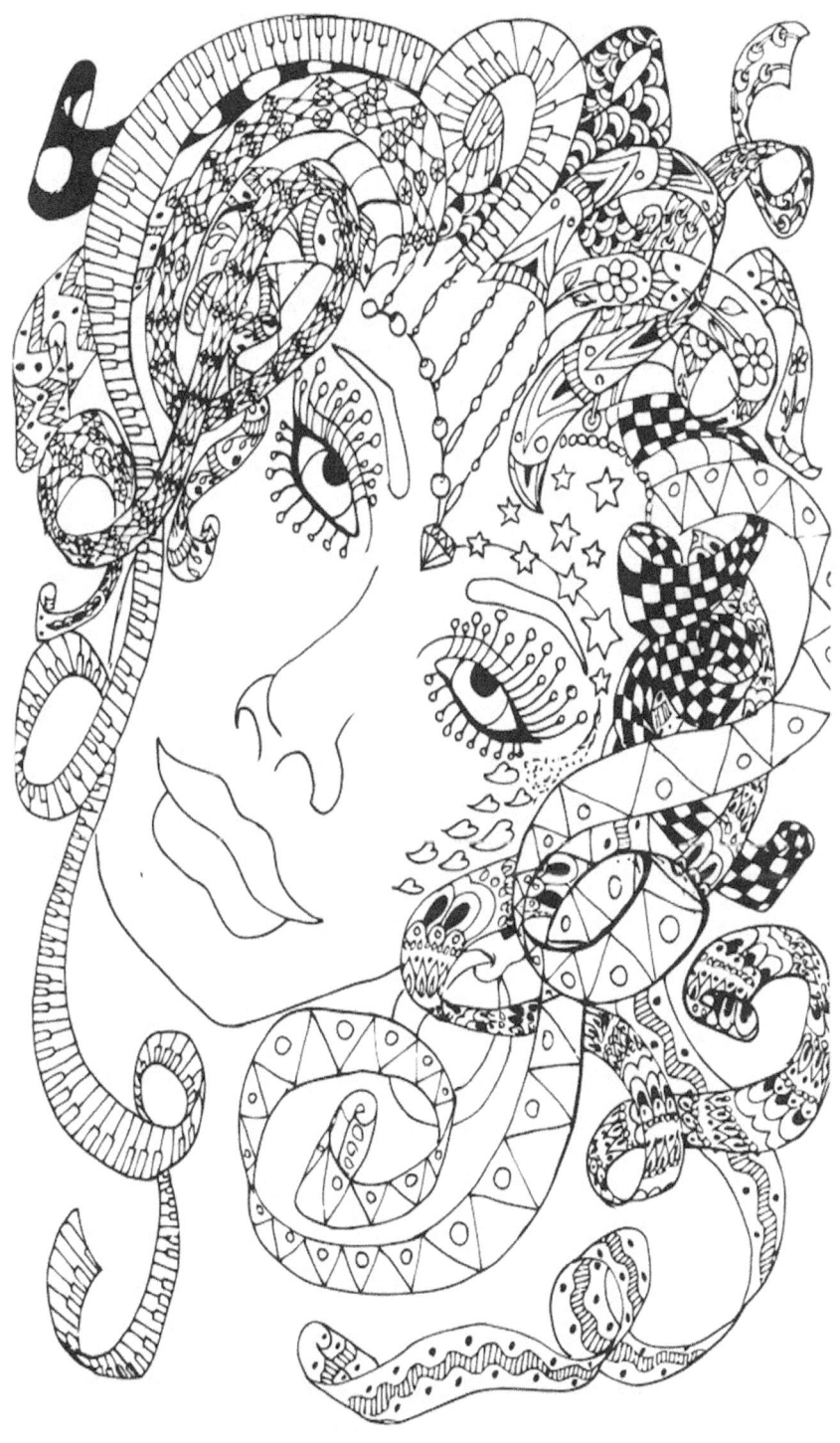

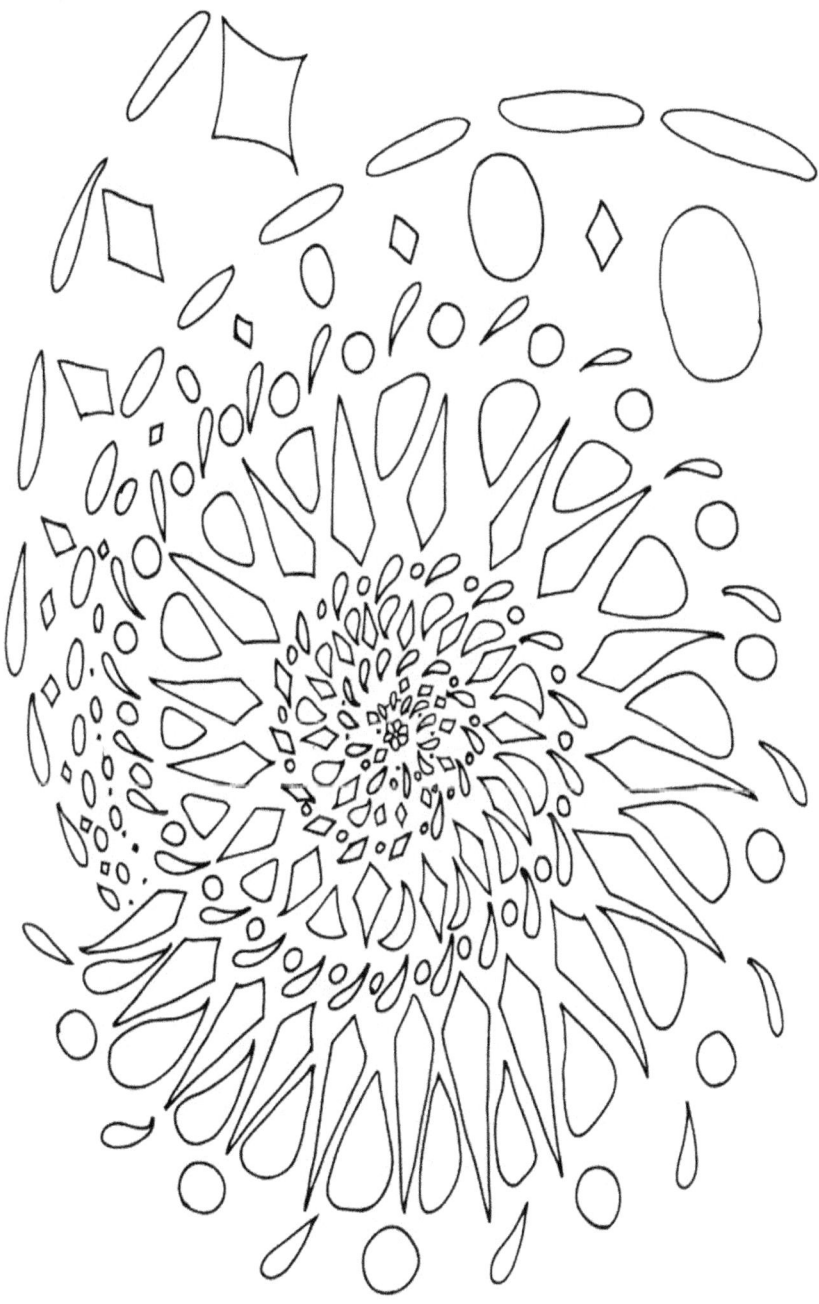

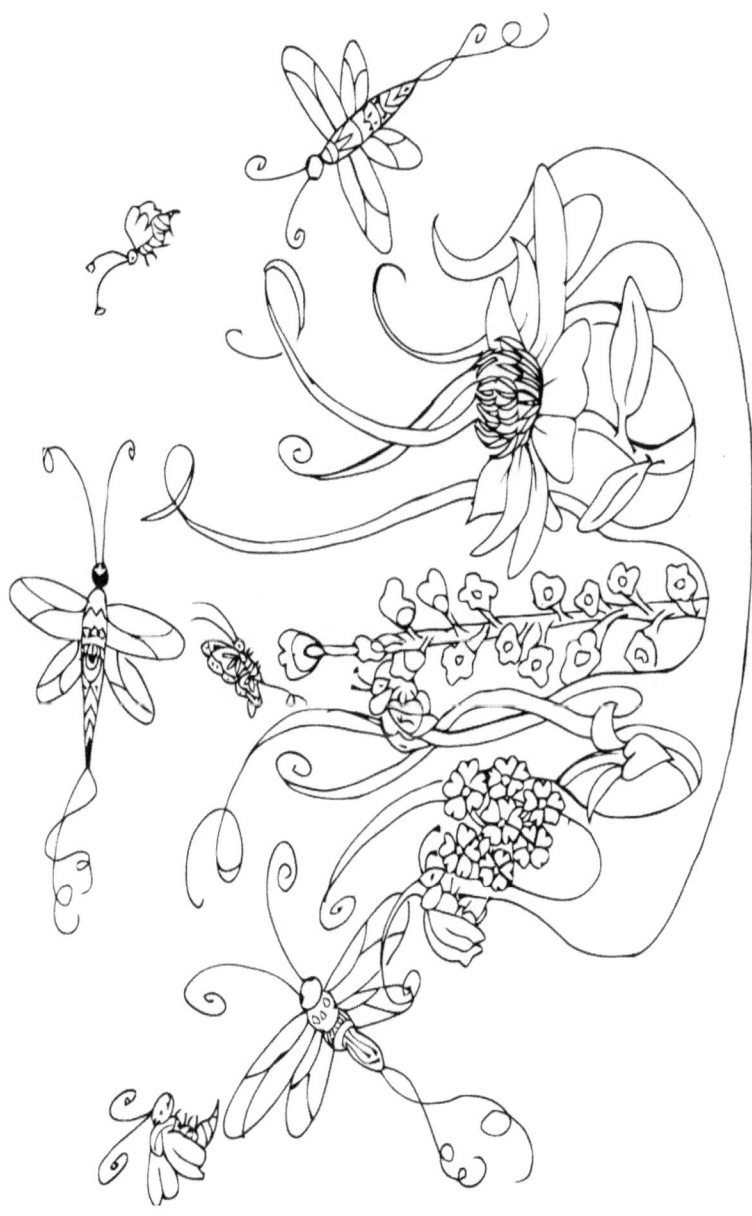

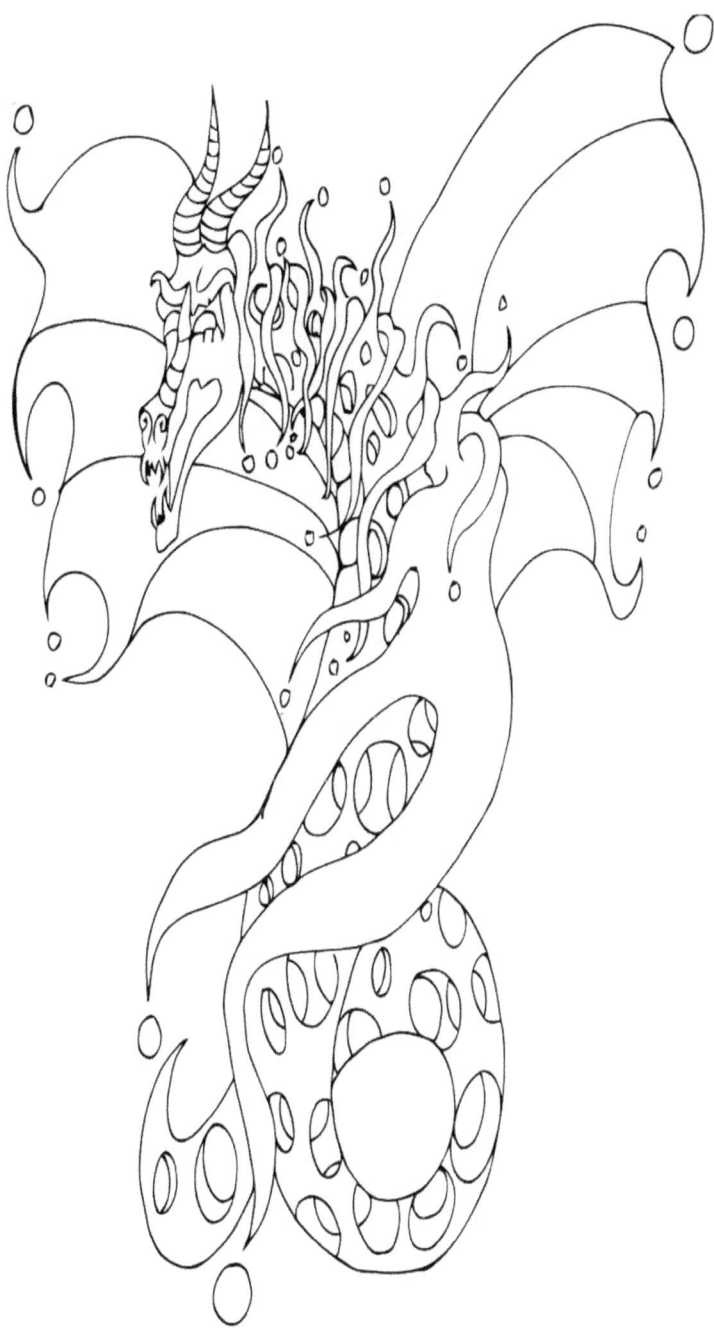

V. PEREIRA

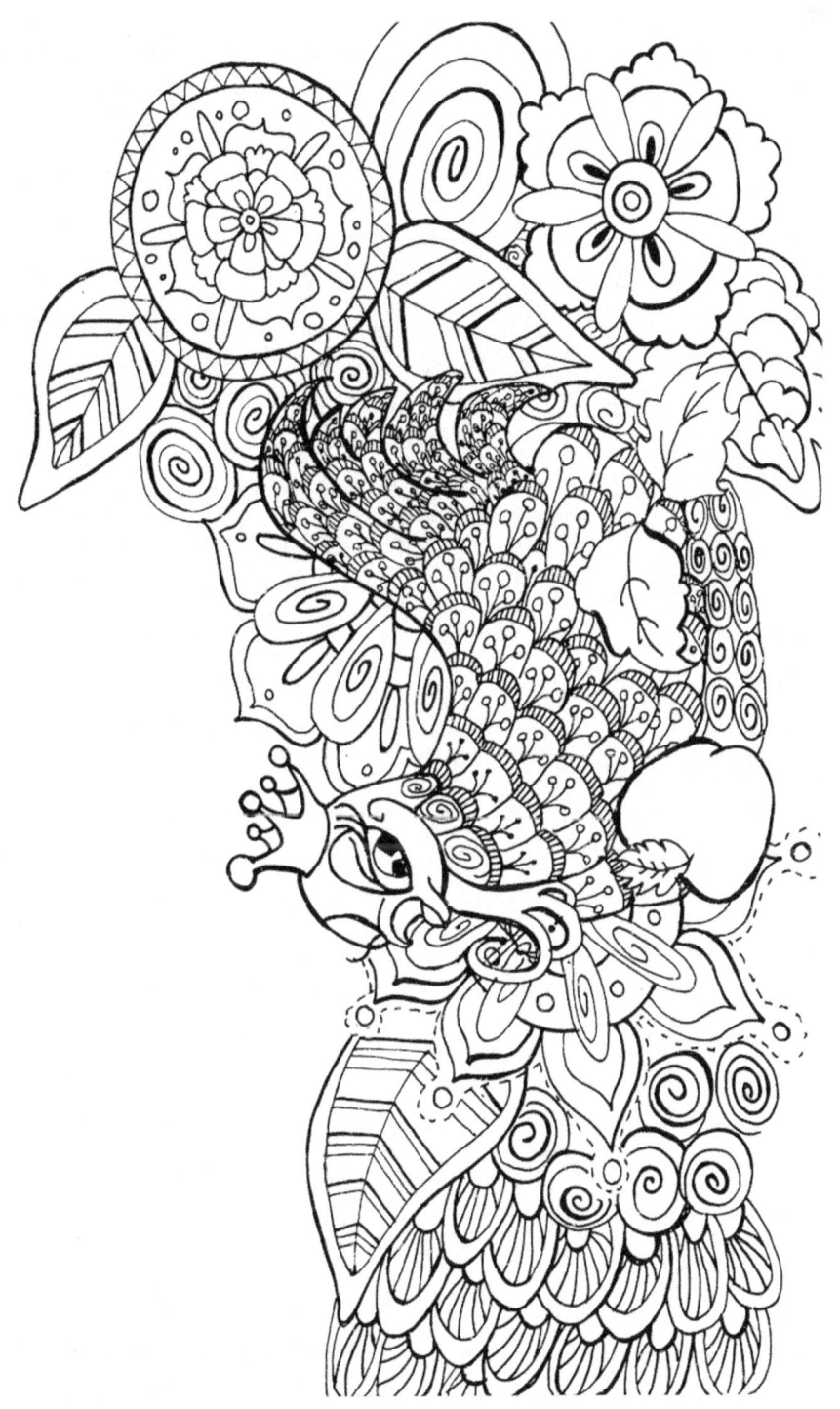

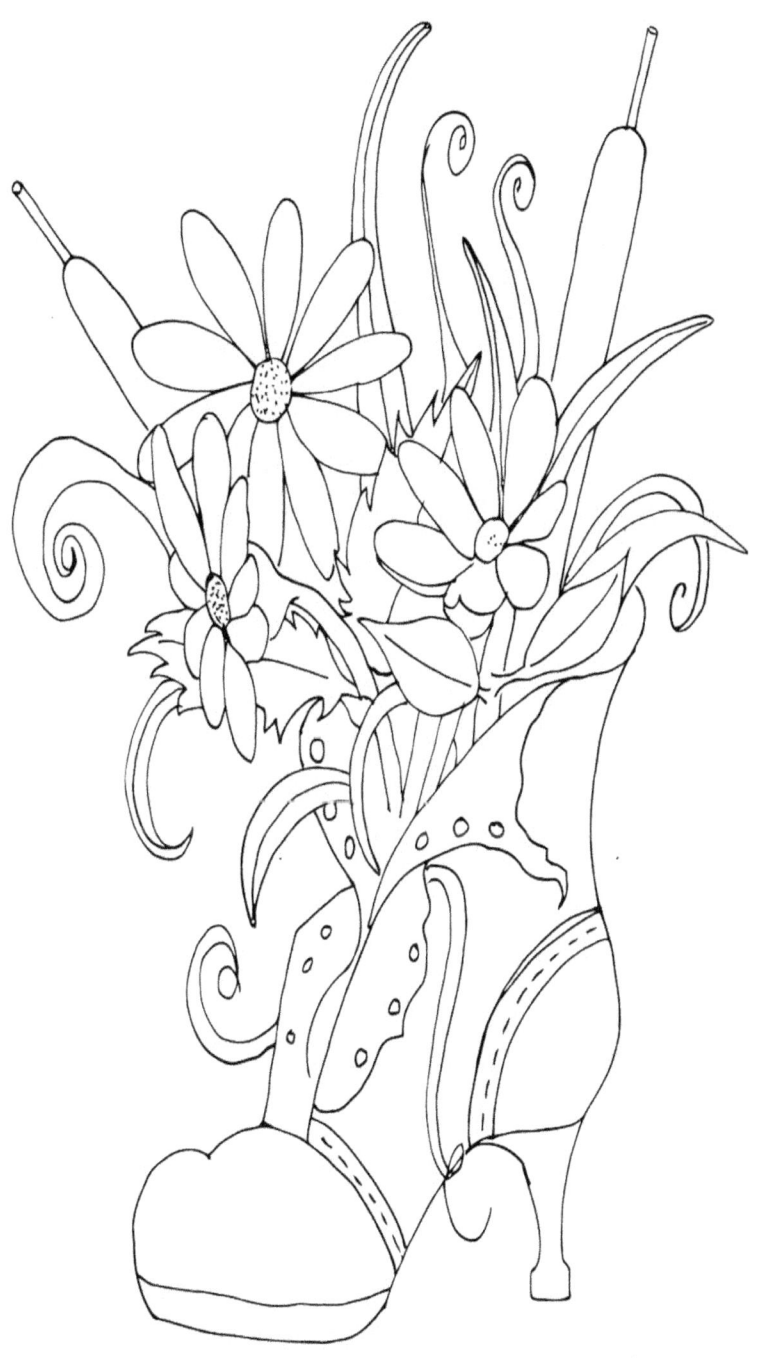

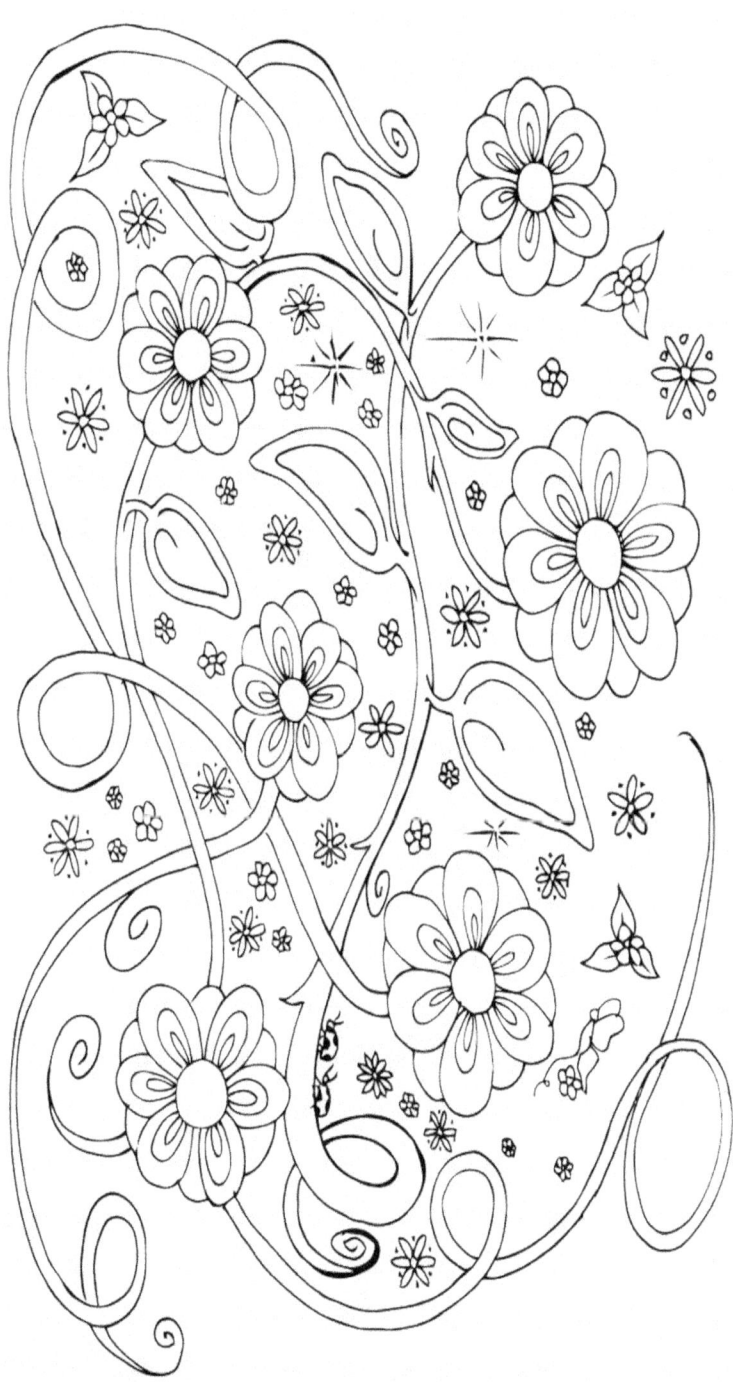

V. PEREIRA

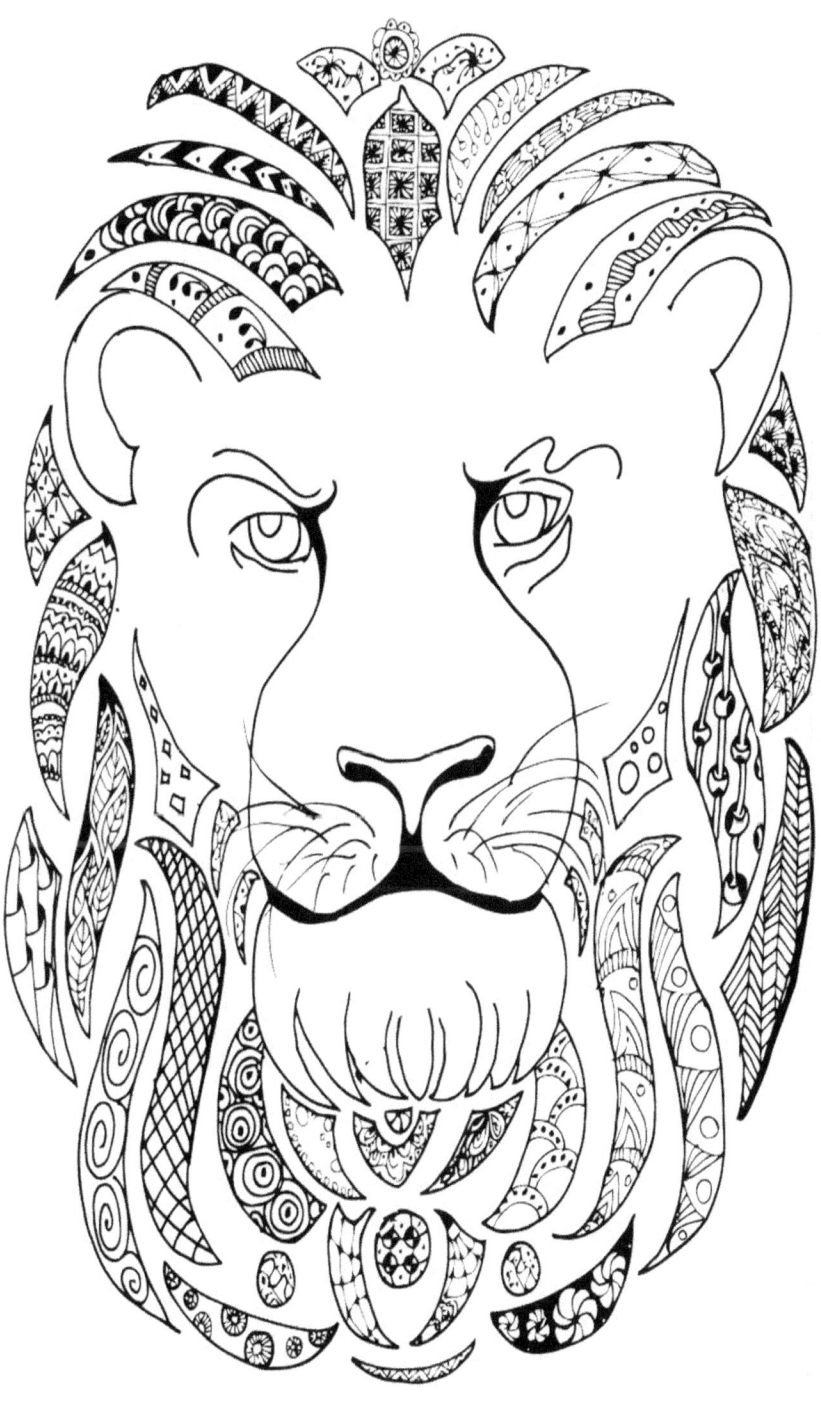

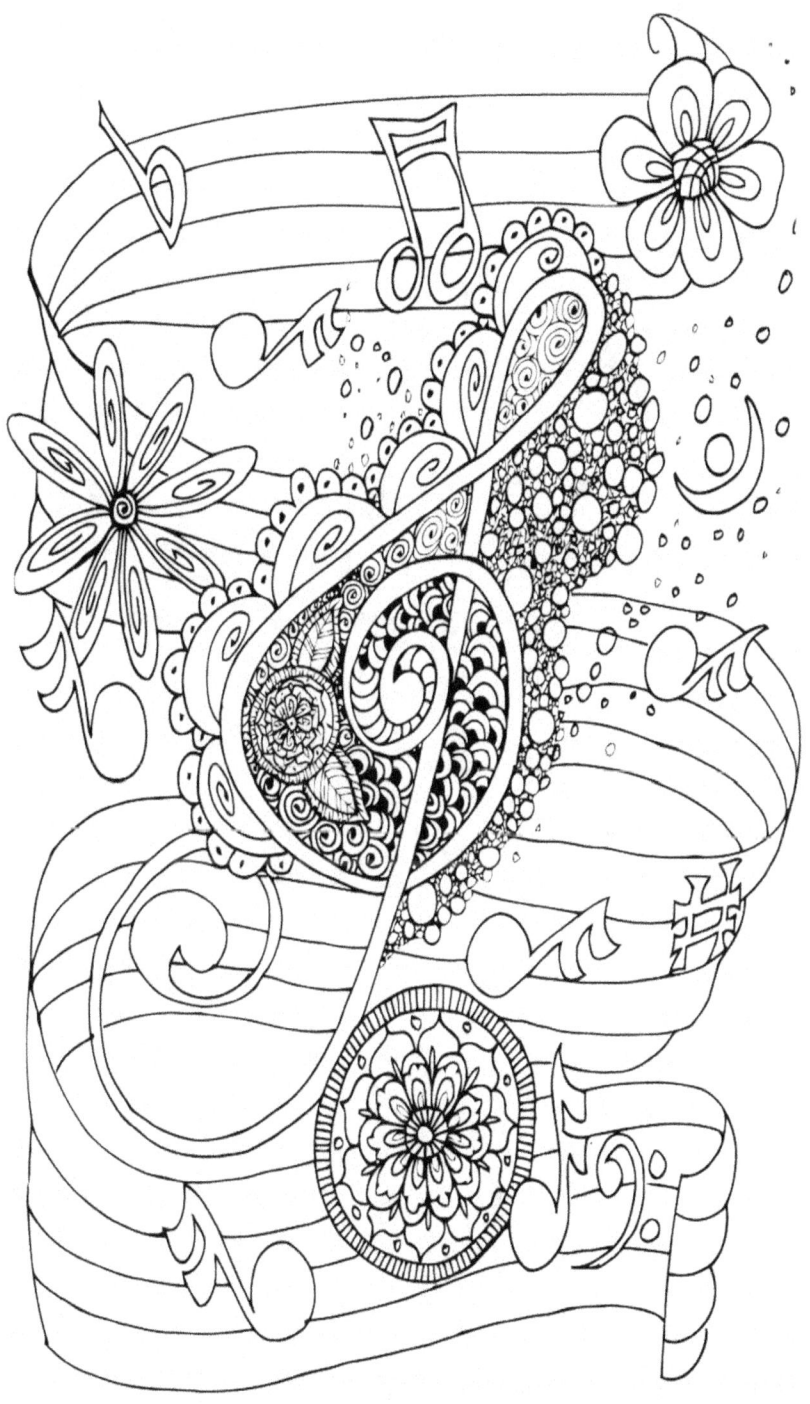

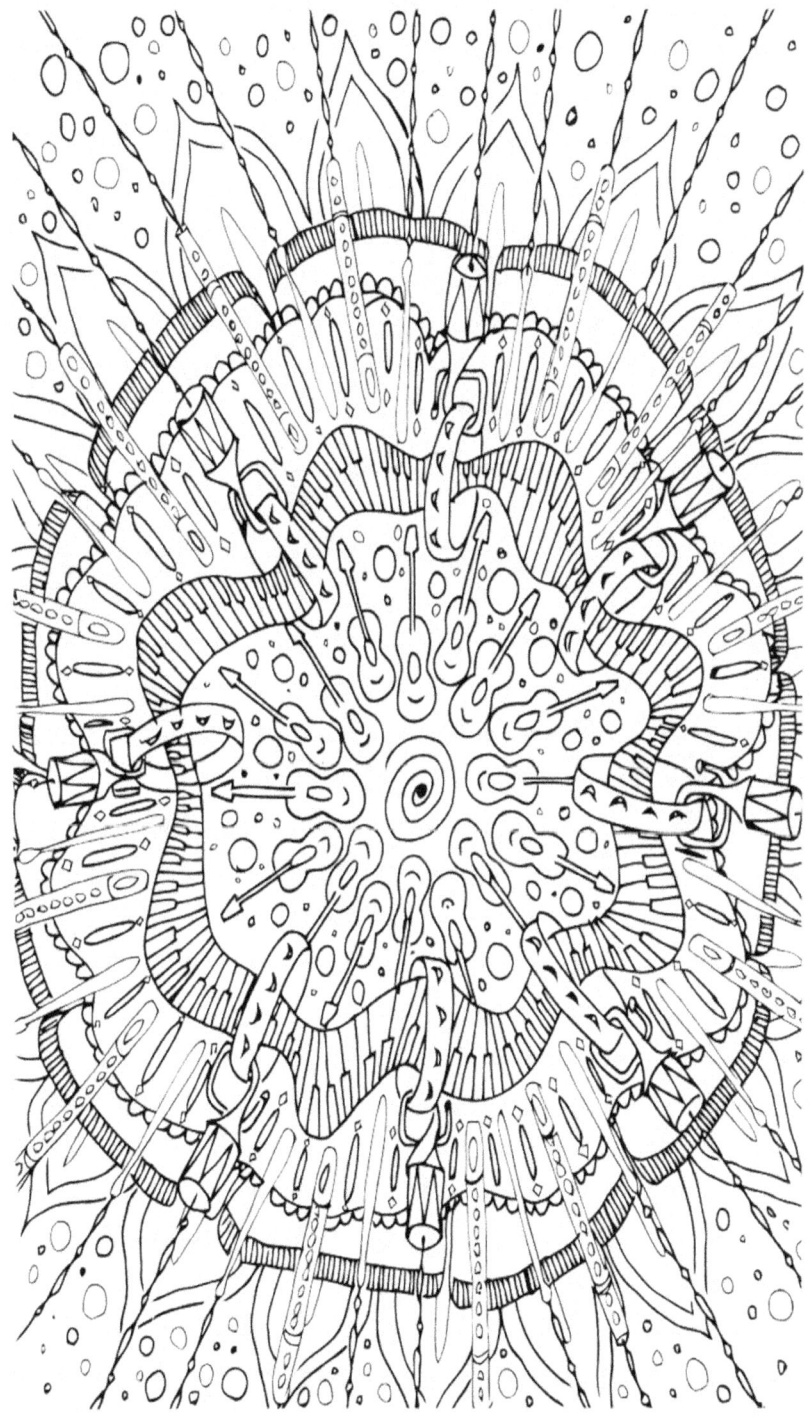

V. PEREIRA

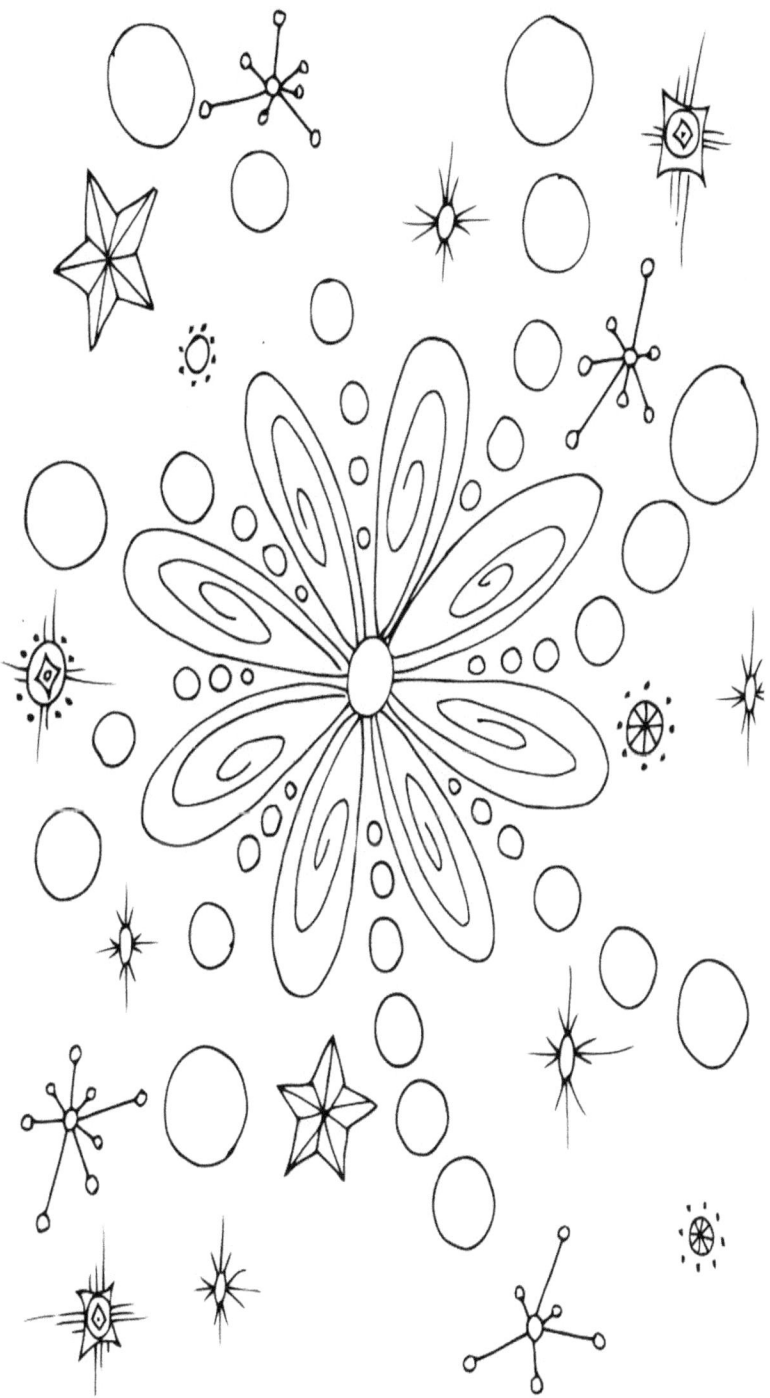

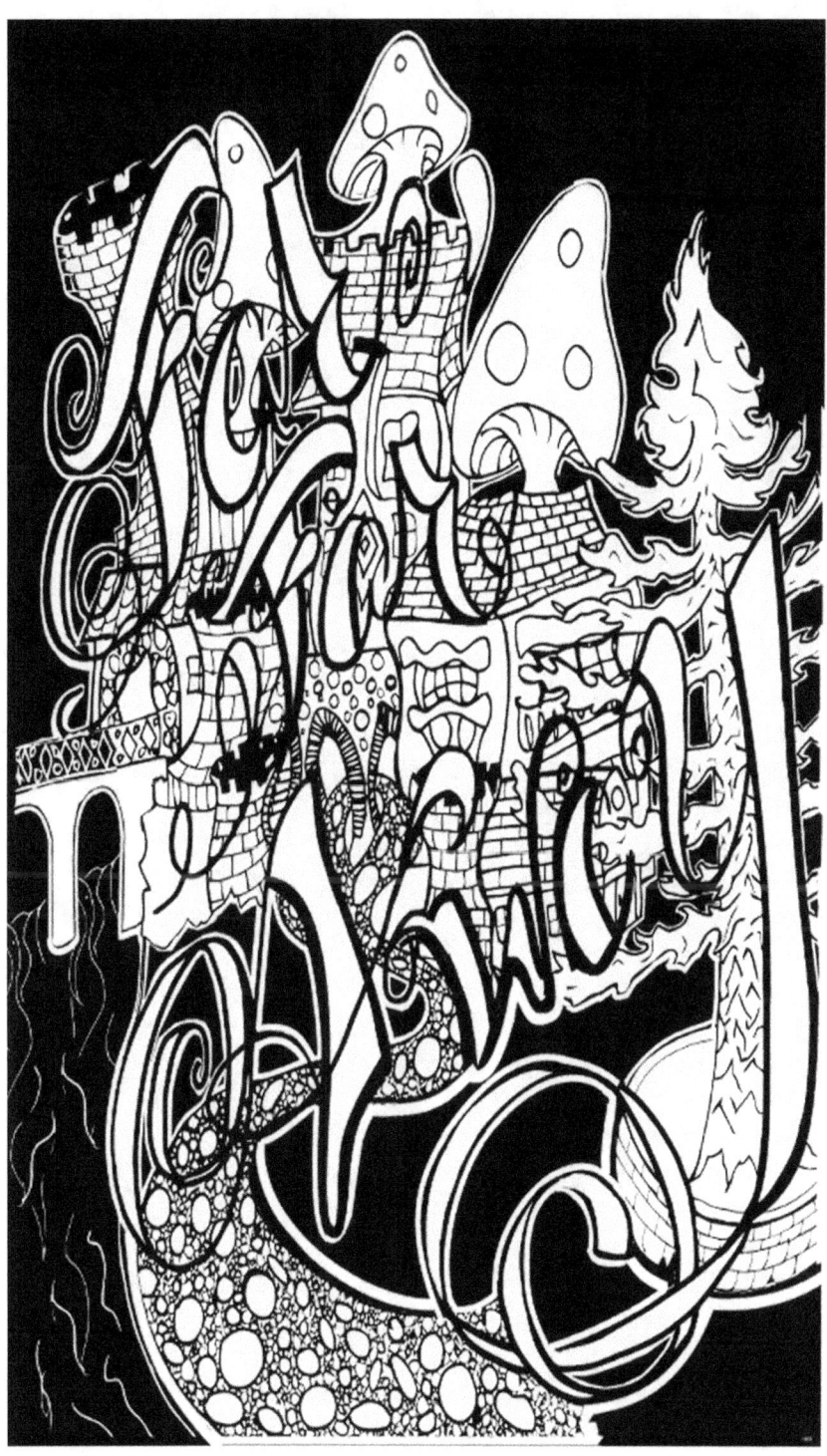

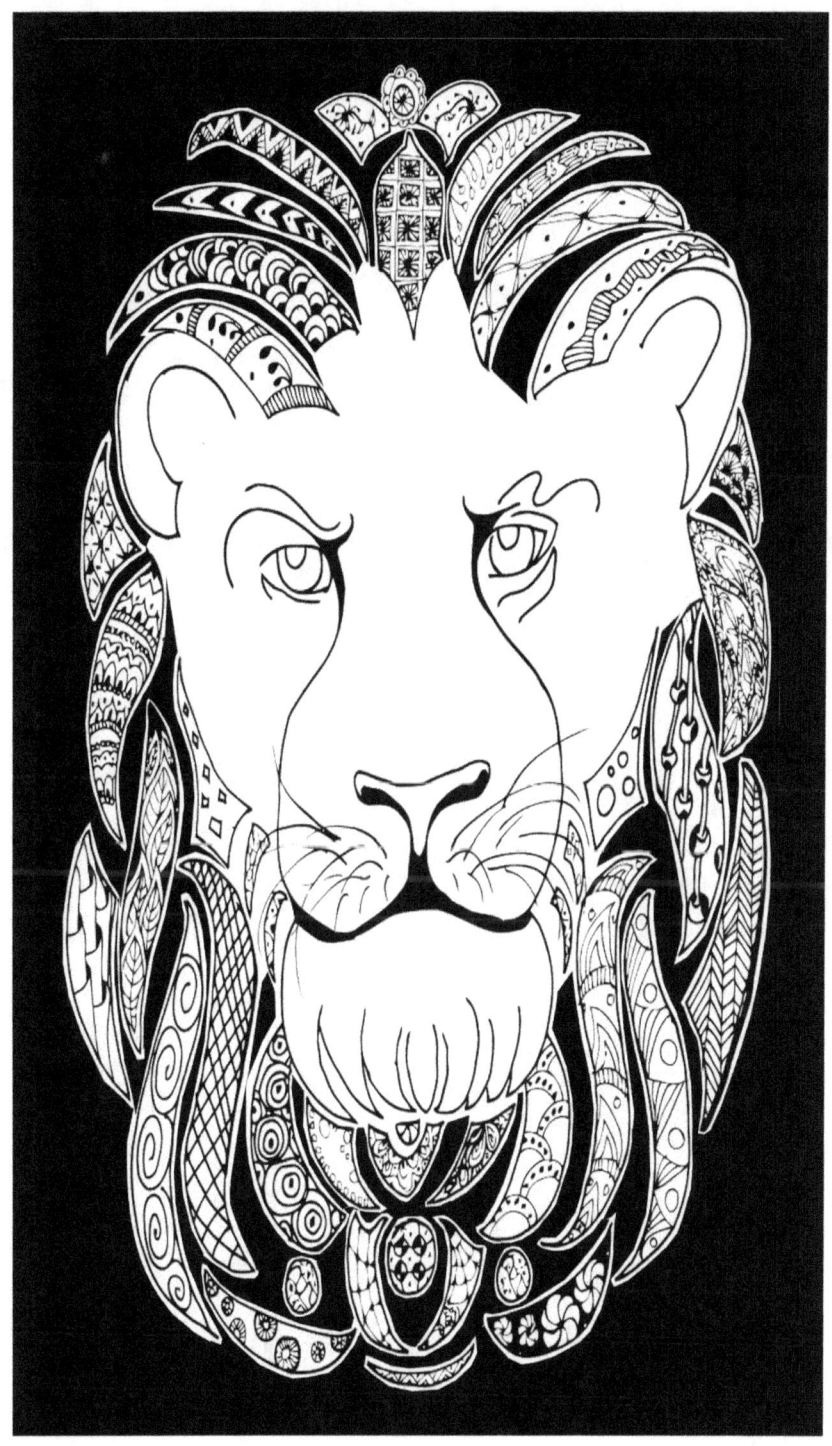

Thanks so much for your support!
Here is where you can find the .pdf file for printing and sharing over and over!

https://auntievs.files.wordpress.com/2016/07/far-away-6-x-9.doc

If you enjoyed this coloring book, please consider stopping by
Auntie V.'s page author page at Amazon and choose
'Far, Far Away -Pocket Edition' to leave a review
http://www.amazon.com/author/auntiev

or just google

'Auntie V.'s Coloring Books for Adults, Far, Far Away'

AUNTIE V.'S OTHER
COLORING BOOKS FOR ADULTS

SERIES 1: AUNTIE V'S ADULT COLORING BOOKS

VOL 1 - DIA DE LOS MUERTOS

VOL 2 - VALENTINES DAY

VOL 3 - GRANNIES SCARVES

VOL 4 - AUNTIE V.'S MANDALAS

SERIES 2: HAND DRAWN WITH LOVE

VOL 1: FAR, FAR AWAY

And please, do tell a friend! :)